Original title:
The Gratitude of Harvest

Copyright © 2024 Creative Arts Management OÜ
All rights reserved.

Author: Vivian Laurent
ISBN HARDBACK: 978-9916-94-364-9
ISBN PAPERBACK: 978-9916-94-365-6

Harvest Moonlight and Heartstrings

Beneath the moon with a wink so bright,
We dance with veggies, leading a sight.
Tomatoes giggle, potatoes prance,
In the garden, we all take a chance.

Cornfields chuckle, the pumpkins roll,
In silly costumes, they play their role.
Carrots wear glasses, all ready to see,
What wacky fun tonight's harvest will be!

The scarecrow grins with his straw-filled glee,
Waving at crows, "Come dance along, please!"
He tells corny jokes, and they caw in cheer,
As they bob and weave, no hint of fear!

Now gathered round with baskets in hand,
We feast on goodies from our merry land.
Cider with humor and pies that wink,
Let's raise a toast to the fruits of our ink!

Each bite is laughter, each sip a jest,
Who knew that carrots would party the best?
So here's to the fall, with silliness ripe,
A joyful harvest, with jokes that type!

The Rhythm of Abundant Days

Cabbages dance, tomatoes jive,
While carrots hum, so alive.
Chickens cluck a silly tune,
Worms do the twist beneath the moon.

Pumpkins wink, they're quite the sight,
Zucchinis wearing hats, oh what a fright!
Lettuce giggles in the breeze,
Corn stalks tapping, 'Do you please?'

Reaping in Harmony

We harvest smiles, it's quite the spree,
With squash and beans singing in glee.
The rake trips over laughing peas,
As radishes tease the bumblebees.

Maize in rows, all lined up neat,
Who knew veggies could dance with such beat?
The scarecrow's got moves, gotta admit,
Doing the cha-cha, not a bit shy of it.

Celebrating Nature's Generosity

Look at the apples, all in a line,
Declaring, 'We're sweet!' Oh how they shine.
Potatoes huddle, avoiding the ruck,
While onions giggle, oh what bad luck.

Sunflowers grin, tall as a kite,
Guess they think they're a real delight.
The herbs are whispering, what's the fuss?
"Who's got the time for a happy bus?"

The Joy of Flourishing Life

Berries chuckle, their sweetness divine,
While broccoli boasts, 'I'm best with wine!'
Radishes leap, in a hop and a skip,
Tomatoes chase flies, what a wild trip!

Green beans giggle, up on their stake,
All while the pumpkins hibernate in cake.
Nature's bounty, a whimsical spree,
Bringing joy, just like a jubilee!

Gifts Wrapped in Leaves

In a field where pumpkins grew,
A scarecrow danced with a chicken too.
They plotted with glee, under the moonlight,
To roast marshmallows and have a bite.

Corn stalks towered like a crazy parade,
While squirrels stole snacks, unafraid.
A haystack party, oh what a sight,
With laughter and jokes, from day till night.

Cherishing Nature's Wealth

Tomatoes juggled in vibrant red,
While carrots whispered secrets instead.
The radish joined in, with a cheeky grin,
Said, 'Don't forget to toss me in!"

Cucumbers stretched like they were in a race,
While lettuce flaunted their leafy lace.
Nature's bounty, a goofy theatre,
With every veggie, a daring meter!

Beyond the Furrows of Gratitude

In gardens lush, old gnomes conspire,
With sunflowers growing ever higher.
They tried to dance but fell with glee,
Turning dirt into comedy!

The carrots rolled in a tumble of hues,
While onions cried, 'We bring the blues!'
Each plot of land, a stage divine,
Where every harvest shares a punchline.

The Blessing of Burgeoning Life

Mashed pumpkins telling tales in the breeze,
While bees buzzed around, feeling at ease.
The lettuce leafed through its favorite book,
While peas peeked out with a curious look.

Apples competed in a game of catch,
While potatoes plotted a sneaky match.
Nature's gifts wrapped in humor tight,
Bringing joy, from morn till night!

Moments of Serene Gratitude

In the field, we danced with glee,
Cornflakes flew, oh, what a spree!
The scarecrow laughed, his hat askew,
While crows watched on—what could they do?

Pumpkins rolled like bouncy balls,
We made them hats, they look like dolls!
The sun shone bright, not a cloud in sight,
We joked, we sang—oh, what a sight!

The Color of Thankfulness

In shades of brown, and patchy green,
A garden grows, like a well-timed scene.
Tomatoes blushed, so ripe and round,
We joked they'd win a beauty crown!

Carrots hiding, like they're shy,
Peeking out, with a little lie.
"We're not veggies!" they shout with glee,
"We're candy in the dirt, you see!"

Seasons of Rich Remembrance

The leaves dance down, a golden show,
We laughed as they fell—what a flow!
Mice in sweaters, counting their cheese,
While squirrels debated—"Who takes the peas?"

Harvest moons and pies so sweet,
The family feasts, a joyful treat.
Uncle Joe's jokes, like corny fries,
Leave us all in fits and sighs.

Harvesting Joy in Every Grain

In grain bins full, a treasure trove,
We counted yields, our laughter wove.
With every scoop, came silly cheer,
"We've got enough to last the year!"

We danced with oats, like silly fools,
Swapping flavors, making rules.
"Is it chocolate?" a friend would say,
We just smiled—what a harvest day!

Flourishing in the Fall

Leaves shift from green to gold,
Squirrels stash their nuts, so bold.
Pumpkins smile, a sight to see,
Got a pie? Just save some for me.

Cider flows like rivers do,
A little spice? Maybe two.
Cornstalks dance in breezy cheer,
Fall's the time to shed a tear.

Jackets on, we stomp the ground,
Crunching leaves, the best sound found.
Sweaters snug, hot cocoa's near,
Harvest time, let's shout, 'Hooray!' here!

Funny hats and outfits bright,
Farmers joke, they feel just right.
Sing of crops and watch 'em grow,
Fall is here, let laughter flow!

Nature's Generous Embrace

Fields are bursting, oh what joy,
Look at that big, round ball named Troy.
Tomatoes blush, they wave hello,
Wave back and feel the warm sun's glow.

Berries tumble from the vine,
Nature's gifts, they taste so fine.
Birds are chirping with delight,
'Gimme seeds!' they squawk, a sight!

Buzzy bees sing, 'All is well,'
Pollen's spreading like a spell.
Flowers laugh, they sway and twirl,
Dancing petals, 'Give it a whirl!'

Nature's teasing, 'Eat some more!'
Gifts from earth, who could ask for more?
Meadows filled with scents divine,
Thank goodness for this life of mine!

A Toast to the Earth's Giving

Raise your glass, let's celebrate,
Fruits and veggies on our plate.
Carrots wiggle, peas all cheer,
Let's make room for pies, oh dear!

Chickens cluck in fancy hats,
"Feathers fly!" the farmer chats.
Toast to greens that grow so tall,
Raise your fork and give a call!

Corn mazes twist like drunken dreams,
Look and find! It's not what it seems.
Sweeter fruit, we've made a mess,
But who cares? We love this fest!

So here's to those who work the land,
With dirt on boots and strong, rough hands.
Let laughter fill the evening air,
With friends around, there's joy to share!

Seasons of Thankful Souls

In the garden, giggles rise,
Pumpkin faces, silly eyes.
Harvest moon in silver light,
Swinging kids, a joyful sight.

Chickens roam, they judge our dance,
Do they think we stand a chance?
Bags of apples, bags galore,
Mom says, 'There's room for more!'

Fall parades with costumes bright,
Squirrels stealing, what a plight!
Giggle at the flopping leaves,
Nature plots while everyone heaves!

Thankful hearts, let's raise a cheer,
To all the crops that brought us here.
Seasons change, but joy remains,
With silly fun in sunny lanes!

Skies Painted with Thankfulness

In fields where produce gathers cheer,
Cabbages nod, they seem to hear.
Tomatoes blush, so ripe and red,
Saying thanks with each little spread.

The pumpkins grin, just look at them,
Waving leaves like a leafy gem.
Cornstalks dance like they're on cue,
Sipping sun, while skies turn blue.

The scarecrow's got a joke or two,
He laughs with crows as they pass through.
Gourd-tastic tales fill the air,
With frolicking veggies, we all share.

So raise a cup of apple juice,
To Mother Earth, we let loose.
With playful spirit, laughter swells,
In our harvest tales, joy dwells.

Giving Thanks to the Earth

In dirt we find a trove of cheer,
Carrots hidden, oh my dear!
With squash that chuckle, round and bright,
They tease the onions, what a sight!

The potatoes peek from earthen beds,
Waving at all with leafy heads.
Beans just laugh, stretching with pride,
As butterflies join in for the ride.

Each turnip whispers, 'What a find!'
Spilling secrets of the kind.
As bees join in this funny show,
Pollinating smiles, to and fro.

So let us toast with pumpkin pie,
With laughter rolling, oh my, my!
For in this bounty, rich and bold,
Are stories worth their weight in gold.

Threads of Abundance Interwoven

Woven in baskets, treasures gleam,
Lettuce giggles, tomatoes beam.
Zucchinis joke about their size,
While eggplants flaunt their purple ties.

Cucumbers cuddle with the vine,
Saying, 'Let's pickle, it'll be divine!'
Radishes roast with a spicy glow,
In this banquet, what a show!

Basil winks with a fragrant grace,
While garlic tells jokes, just in case.
Corn on the cob joins the fun,
Sipping sunshine until it's done.

So gather 'round, on this good day,
With veggies leading the parade play.
In every bite, a hearty laugh,
Life's harvest joy, our funniest half.

A Harvest for the Heart

With baskets full of giggly glee,
We stumble home, just wait and see.
Squash on wheels, what a delight,
Rolling down the path, oh what a sight!

Garlic's breath, a pungent charm,
While beans jive, causing no harm.
Tomatoes bouncing like rubber balls,
In this garden, everyone calls.

Spinach grins with leafy might,
Spreading joy, so green and bright.
Peas in pods are in a race,
Giggling as they find their place.

So join this feast, with smiles to spare,
For every nibble, joy's laid bare.
In every morsel, laughter's art,
We toast this bounty, warm in heart.

We'll Sow What We've Reaped

In the field of chuckles where veggies grow,
We planted some jokes and watched them glow.
Potatoes with sneakers, carrots that dance,
Every time we harvest, we take a chance.

A tomato in sunglasses, so cool and bright,
Claims it's the best in the garden tonight.
With peppers that giggle and squash that grins,
We sow laughter, hoping fun begins.

Corn kernels gossip, they twist and they twirl,
While beans do the cha-cha, oh what a whirl!
As we gather our bounty, we can't help but cheer,
For laughter and veggies make the best of the year.

So here's to the harvest, both silly and sweet,
We've reaped a good time, now let's hit repeat.

Celebrating the Seasons' Gifts

The seasons bring gifts we can't quite explain,
Like broccoli nightmares and pumpkin rain.
A carrot wore glasses, quite smart, it would seem,
While radishes plotted to take over the dream.

With apples doing tango and pears that can sing,
We dance in the orchard, it's quite the wild fling.
Lettuce flails wildly with a leafy delight,
Each harvest brings joy, oh what a sight!

In the meadow of mischief, the mirth takes its turn,
As garlic gives hugs, and onions just yearn.
We toss out the worries, let's feast on the fun,
For the seasons bring gifts, and we've only begun!

So here's to the laughter, the quirks and the play,
In the bounty we gather, let's embrace the ballet.

Echoes of a Plentiful Heart

In a garden where giggles echo and sing,
A squash with a crown thinks it's royalty bling.
Tomatoes are shouting, "We're juicier than you!"
While beans form a band, and they're starting to brew.

Each carrot has stories of soil and of sun,
Whispering secrets of laughter and fun.
Radishes blushing, all dressed in their red,
They share little tales as we laugh till we're fed.

With herbs full of wisdom that tickle the nose,
And onions that chuckle, oh how it all flows!
The echoes of joy are planted right here,
In the bounty we gather, let laughter draw near.

Together we'll feast on the fruits of the jest,
With hearts full of laughter, we truly are blessed.

A Cornucopia of Kindness

In a basket of chuckles where friendships abound,
A melon will joke with its friends all around.
An apple's sweet grin as it winks with delight,
Makes oranges giggle throughout the night.

Celery whispers, "Bite me, I'm crunchy!" so loud,
While broccoli giggles, quite proud of its crowd.
In this cornucopia, kindness does flow,
As vegetables prance in a bright, joyful show.

They bake up some pies filled with humor and cheer,
Sharing slices of laughter, oh, bring everyone near!
The pumpkin parade rolls with hats of pure glee,
It's a feast of good spirits, just come share with me.

So let's raise our forks high, give a cheer for the zest,
In this cornucopia, we're truly the best!

The Golden Grain of Thanks

In fields of gold, we dance and sway,
With silly hats, we shout hooray!
The corn's so tall, it's lost its plot,
We plant our seeds, and all but rot!

Oh pumpkins round, with smiles so bright,
They laugh and roll in pure delight!
We sing to beans, oh what a treat,
While veggies hum a harvest beat!

Potatoes play hide and seek all day,
In mounds of dirt, oh what a fray!
Carrots poke heads, they think they're wise,
But we just giggle at their surprise!

So raise your cups filled with fresh cider,
As squirrels in hats get even wider!
When nature gives, we laugh and cheer,
With funny friends, the harvest's here!

Tribute to the Yielding Land

Oh yielding land, with gifts galore,
You make us laugh, then beg for more!
With apples plump and squashes round,
Our tummies grumble at the sound!

Beets try to dance, they twist and shout,
But fall right down, oh what a clout!
The broccoli counts, one, two, three,
It trips and bounces off a tree!

The onions cry, but not from pain,
Just too much joy from all the grain!
And as we gather, oh what glee,
A harvest party, just you and me!

So lift your voice, let laughter flow,
In fields of plenty, laughs will grow!
To all the lands, we give a cheer,
For laughter shared, we hold so dear!

Pouring Forth from Nature's Cup

Nature's cup spills joy and cheer,
With every bite, we spread good beer!
From fruity peels to veggie tails,
Each scoop is full of silly tales!

Jam jars dance like they're on stage,
Spreading sweetness, oh what a rage!
The syrup drips with a giggly sound,
While pancakes flip, not quite round!

The lettuce winks, the cucumbers grin,
As farmers play games of hide and seek in!
With every seed sown with care,
We giggle hard at the weeds' despair!

So let's raise glasses to nature's fun,
To all the laughter that we've spun!
Filled with cheer, we say hooray,
For every harvest is a funny buffet!

When Life Grows Rich

When life is rich, we start to play,
With every pea, we shout hooray!
The carrots boast, their tops held high,
While sunflowers reach toward the sky!

Beans tell jokes, they crack us up,
As potatoes swirl in a dancing cup!
The harvest moon starts to giggle,
Beneath its light, we all do wiggle!

Tomatoes blush, not from the sun,
But from the compliments that are just too fun!
Corn on the cob, with buttered cheer,
Will dance around, oh what a sheer!

So when life grows, let's spread the joy,
To little girls and every boy!
In gardens lush, with laughter stitched,
We reap the smiles, all deeply enriched!

A Symphony of Soil and Sun

In fields where veggies dance and play,
The carrots sing, come join their fray!
The sunbeams shine on corn so high,
While potatoes wink from earth nearby.

Beets wear coats of dirt and charm,
And broccoli brings a leafy calm.
With every sprout, there's laughter loud,
As rabbits cheer from their green crowd.

Tomatoes toss in juicy glee,
While peppers throw a spicy spree!
The earth's a stage for green delight,
Where tastiness takes to the light.

So grab a fork, it's time to feast,
On nature's wonders, not the least!
With every bite, a giggle bursts,
As we toast to soil and sun rehearsed!

The Gift of Gathering

With baskets full of nature's loot,
We race the bugs to find our fruit.
A daisy's hat hides in the patch,
While squishy squash gives quite a match.

The apples shout, 'We're ripe, hooray!'
While pumpkins plan their grand buffet.
In every nook, a treasure breeds,
As laughter grows amidst the weeds.

Oh, farmers dance with glee and cheer,
For every sprout brings joy near here!
With hiccuping beans that leap about,
Nature chuckles, without a doubt.

So gather round, let's pick and share,
A feast of fun beyond compare!
With every sprig, a silly prank,
As gratitude flows from nature's tank!

Relishing the Reap

The harvest comes, let's raise a cheer,
With pumpkins grand and vision clear.
Carrots peek with a grin so wide,
And laughter sparks from every side.

Kale does a jig in the morning sun,
While peas roll laughter, oh what fun!
Zucchini bounces, all spruced and bright,
As we revel in this tasty sight.

Corn kernels pop like jolly jokes,
As cider flows with merry folks.
With each sweet bite, a chuckle sounds,
As nature's bounty spins around.

So grab your forks, let's dig in deep,
With every slice, a giggle to keep!
As flavors burst, our hearts will leap,
Relishing in a harvest sweep!

When Nature Smiles

When nature smiles, the veggies sing,
The pumpkins bounce with joy in spring.
Fields frolic with laughter all around,
As sprouts unleash their jolly sound.

Radishes giggle as they pop,
While happy onions dance and hop.
Even garlic bulbs tune in to play,
Spicing up our harvest day!

Potato pranks beneath the soil,
As nature plots to make us toil.
But with a harvest, who could frown?
With laughter brewing in our town.

So let's embrace this fruitful spree,
With nature's gifts, so wild and free!
With every bite and every cheer,
We'll celebrate the humor here!

Gifts of the Seasons' End

Leaves are falling, oh what a sight,
Pumpkins grinning with all their might.
Cider flows, the apples cheer,
Hope I don't trip on the last beer!

Squirrels stash away their treats,
While I'm just seeking warm eats.
Harvest dance, we sway around,
Stomping puddles, what a sound!

Corn stalks waving, say hi to me,
"Did you really plant us?" they tease with glee.
I planted once, they all took flight,
Just like my hopes for that pie tonight!

So gather 'round, we all can share,
With smiley faces, and a little flair.
Fill your plates, do not delay,
Ride the fun, it's harvest play!

The Flavor of Abundance

Tomatoes blushing, ripe and round,
Hiding underneath the leafy mound.
With every bite, a surprise or two,
I'll slip on juice, it's true, oh boo!

Garlic's scent fills the sunny air,
I cooked too much, now I must share.
"Oh come and taste," I call to the crew,
They run away—oops, did I say stew?

Beets are purple, carrots are bright,
Toss them all in for a colorful bite!
"Eat your veggies," my mama said,
Now I'm a grown-up, just slip into bed.

Dinner's done, but leftovers remain,
Fridge's a circus, can't feel my brain.
What was for lunch? A mystery feast,
Oh well, cheers to that and a harvest beast!

Sheltered by Mother Earth

Beneath the soil, a party awaits,
Roots are dancing—oh, what fun fates!
Potatoes giggle as they join in,
"Hope you find us—it's time to spin!"

Under the sun, let's not delay,
We gather goodies in a quirky way.
Onions cry while carrots parade,
Getting muddy is how joy is made!

"Let's play hide and seek," says the corn,
With popped-up hair, it's surely worn.
Dig deep and discover what's below,
Pushing up flowers with a vibrant glow!

So rejoice in the harvest, no need to pout,
Even if next week, it's just takeout.
Grow a laugh, let the stories unfurl,
Nature's humor makes the world swirl!

From Field to Heart

Here come the veggies, fresh and bold,
A friendly squash with stories told.
Got a cart that's overflowing fast,
Hope these greens really last!

Zucchini rolling down the lane,
Just a hop, it's in the rain!
"Don't squish me," the peppers shout,
They're having fun, without a doubt!

Basil and thyme all compete for space,
"Pick us first, we're full of grace!"
I grab them all, why take just one?
Cooking frenzy—just pure fun!

Pasta simmering with herbs so bright,
"I'm a chef!" I claim with delight.
Friends at the table, laughter's the goal,
A plate of joy warms the heart and soul.

Fields Illuminated with Thanks

In fields so bright, the veggies sway,
With carrots boasting, 'We saved the day!'
Tomatoes blush in the golden light,
While pumpkins giggle, 'What a sight!'

The corn on high starts telling jokes,
Like 'What did one ear say to the folks?'
They chuckle loud, a mazy sound,
As nature's humor spins around.

Beets wear shades, feeling quite cool,
Radishes dance, breaking every rule.
The harvest smiles, all green and gold,
In this circus, laughter unfolds.

So let's raise a glass to veggies grand,
With pies and stews, a feast so planned.
With laughter bright and plates piled high,
In our funny fields, we dream and sigh.

A Dance of Abundance

In the orchard, apples swirl and twirl,
While pear trees giggle, their branches unfurl.
'What a party!' the sunflower shouts,
As bees come buzzing, dancing about.

Pumpkins waltz in shiny attire,
Zucchinis slip on stage, never tire.
With squash and beans showing off their moves,
It's a harvest ball that surely grooves!

The fruit flies buzz in a silly spree,
'Join the dance, don't you want to be free?'
With great big grins, the veggies cheer,
As every bite brings joy, oh dear!

So swing around, let laughter grow,
In nature's dance, we steal the show.
From the vine to the plate, a wild romance,
A celebration of life, in every chance.

Nature's Generosity Unfurled

A bounty bright, with giggles and grins,
Chickens cluck, wearing tiny chins.
The carrots shout, 'We've done our best!'
While beans play hopscotch, a silly quest.

Crowded fields do a merry jig,
As radishes puff and the squash gets big.
Gone are the troubles of earlier strife,
As nature dishes out a comical life!

Little ladybugs cheer and clap,
As cucumbers slide down for a nap.
Tomatoes squish, in playful defeat,
While pumpkins plan their next retreat.

So here's to the gifts that grow each day,
With laughter and joy in a colorful way.
Let's feast and giggle, raise a toast,
For nature's humor, we love the most!

Beneath the Weight of Bounty

Beneath heavy branches, fruits hang down,
Grapes exchange jests, wearing a crown.
The harvest hums, 'We're here to play!'
As veggies say, 'Hip-hip-hooray!'

The squash holds court, a comical seat,
While beans plot schemes, oh so sweet.
Potatoes whisper, 'I feel so grand!'
As peppers giggle, forming a band.

In the cool breeze, the corn does tease,
'Take a bite, if you please!'
With pies on the window, a glorious view,
While fruits make a mess, and we all accrue.

So let's cherish the spills, the fun and the mess,
In this joyful harvest, oh, nothing less!
With laughter and love in every bite,
Beneath the weight of bounty, all's just right.

Treasures of Rooted Reflection

In the garden where veggies take a stand,
With carrots and radishes, quite unplanned.
Tomatoes sing songs, all red and round,
While beans do their jig, all over the ground.

Potatoes hide secrets, buried so deep,
They whisper at night when the world's fast asleep.
Zucchini grows wild, it needs a good hug,
Claiming the title of 'vegetable rug.'

Cucumbers giggle in their wobbly suits,
Telling tall tales about garden roots.
Nestled in soil with worms for a friend,
A rollicking harvest that never does end!

So here's to our treasures, so silly and green,
In the dance of the dirt, oh what a scene!
With every odd plant and each funny little sprout,
Let's cheer for the harvest, though we may pout!

Radiant Grains of Appreciation

Wheat waves a hand in the afternoon light,
Saying, 'Let's bake bread, it'll be quite a sight!'
Barley joins in, with a laugh and a grin,
'We'll make breakfast together, let's do it again!'

Corn wears a crown, all yellow and bright,
Making popcorn for movies, a delicious delight.
Sorghum is sweet, with a syrupy smile,
While oats strut around, in a breakfasting style.

Rice takes a dip, splashing all around,
Singing to plants about growing from ground.
Millet joins in, a small grain with big dreams,
Creating a dance full of giggles and beams.

So here's to the grains, with their radiant charms,
They tickle our tummies and wrap us in arms!
With bowls overflowing, let's share with a cheer,
For each grain that whispers, 'I'm glad I'm here!'

Whispers Between the Rows

Between the tall stalks where laughter can bloom,
Radishes giggle in the dark of the gloom.
Onions, they cry, but it's all in good fun,
As they peel away layers, under the sun.

Beans climb up poles, like kids on a swing,
Chasing each other, what joy they can bring!
Peas in their pods are a duo of glee,
Sharing their jokes as sweet as can be.

Lettuce is crisp with a crunchy wise way,
Pointing to veggies, 'Eat fresh every day!'
While garlic, the bold one with quite the strong breath,
Claims he's the hero, in the tale of the chef.

So listen real close as the garden confides,
With humor and spirit, it freely provides.
A playful reminder, amidst nature's prose,
Is laughter abounds in the rows we compose!

Colors of Cornucopia

In a basket of colors, oh what a sight,
Fruits gather 'round, each one a delight.
Apples are rosy, with stories to tell,
While oranges joke, 'We're citrusy as well!'

Grapes wear their outfits of purple and green,
Sipping on sunshine, oh so pristine.
Bananas slip by with a flamboyant chat,
Saying, 'Life's better when you're wearing a hat!'

Berries all giggle, with splashes of hue,
Creating a ruckus when they tumble askew.
Pineapple's knobby, a crown to bestow,
Singing a tune, from the top to below.

So gather your colors, with laughter in tow,
Celebrate nature, let the good vibes flow!
In the cornucopia's joyful embrace,
We feast on chuckles, and love every taste!

Reaping Joy from the Soil

In the garden, I found a potato,
Hiding well, just like a stealthy mate-o.
I dug it up with a glee-filled cheer,
Now it's mashed and cozy, never fear.

Beets rolled in, looking quite profound,
In their purple coats, they danced around.
They sang a tune of sweet delight,
As I chopped them up, oh what a sight!

Carrots plotted in their underground lair,
Popped up smiling like they just don't care.
I said, 'You're crunchy!' They winked with grace,
Now they're in my salad, taking their place.

Corn stood tall, with a cheeky grin,
Claiming it's golden, the best place to begin.
I whispered secrets in hushed delight,
As I buttered them up on a summer night.

Sunlit Fields of Appreciation

In the sun-drenched fields where we play,
Tomatoes blushed, saying, 'Hey, hey!'
They squashed my dreams 'bout being so sweet,
Now they're salsa, a spicy treat!

Pumpkins roll like clowns in a spree,
Wobbling through vibrant orange jubilee.
I cracked a joke, they laughed along,
Now they're pie, oh how they've grown strong!

Zucchini strutted with a green parade,
Thinking of all the cookies they made.
I said, 'You're baked!' they shook and shivered,
Now in my oven, they happily quivered.

With sunflowers nodding, sending a wink,
They gathered the sunlight, more than you think.
Each petal a cheer, each seed a bow,
Showing us joy that we all can know!

The Abundance of Thankful Days

In a cornfield dance, the husks took flight,
With every crunch, it felt just right.
'We're worth our weight!' they squeaked with glee,
And popped like popcorn, wild and free.

Rattling peppers in a spicy haste,
Said, 'Don't you dare let us go to waste!'
I chuckled, 'You're bold and pack a punch,'
Now you're in my salad, part of my lunch!

Onions in layers, so full of tears,
Yet when I chop them, it's laughter, not fears.
They said, 'Crying's just how we show we care,'
Now they're in stew, a savory pair!

Garlic's so fragrant, with a wink and a clove,
'You need us for charm!' they proudly drove.
Together we feast, at the table we sit,
Thanking the veggies, they're a hit!

Nature's Gift Basket

Baskets piled high with veggies galore,
Beans in pajamas, what wisdom they bore.
'We've lived our lives all snug in the dirt,'
Now they're in chili, who knew they'd flirt?

Radishes blushed, with tops standing tall,
'We're not just roots, we can party for all!'
I tossed one up, it rolled in delight,
Now it's a crunch in my stir-fry tonight!

Garlic and chives would gossip and tease,
Whispering spices on a summer breeze.
'We're rich in flavor, you can't just spit,'
Blending with butter, what a perfect fit!

With every pick, my laughter grows wide,
In nature's harvest, there's nothing to hide.
Each quirky veggie with tales to tell,
In this funny feast, I know them so well!

Bounty of the Heart

The autumn wind starts to play,
Rustling leaves in a cheeky way.
Pumpkins roll with a giggling sound,
While apples tumble to the ground.

Chill in the air, the squirrels debate,
"Who gets the acorn that looks just great?"
The harvest moon shines with its glow,
Inside our hearts, warmth starts to flow.

Chili peppers prank in fiery jest,
Competing for who's the very best.
Nature's gifts piled up high,
Bringing laughter, oh my, oh my!

Fragrant pies fill the chilly night,
As critters scurry, quite a sight.
With every bite, our hearts do sing,
Autumn's humor is a joyful thing!

The Blessings in Bounty

In fields where pumpkins start to grow,
The squirrels plot, oh what a show!
With singing crows and clucking cries,
Corn stalks dance 'neath sunny skies.

Oh, what a mess they make each year,
With veggies lost, it's quite the cheer!
Tomatoes fly like Frisbees tossed,
In gardens rich, no chance is lost.

The harvest moon gives quite a grin,
It watches as we tuck in thin.
With pies and jams stacked high with glee,
A feast of flaws, just let it be!

So when the veggies take their bow,
We laugh aloud, it's chaos now!
For in each bite, there's joy to claim,
With every crunch, it's all a game!

Fields of Abundant Harmony

In the fields where clovers bloom,
Bees chase each other, buzzing room.
Chickens strut with feathered pride,
While peas leap from their pods to hide.

Gardens bursting, what a sight,
Radishes racing, oh so bright!
Gourds rolling, trying to win,
The funniest show, let the fun begin!

Lettuce leaves act like a throne,
While pickles promise they won't moan.
In every basket, a quirky face,
Food critters join the silly race!

So here's to all who sow and reap,
With laughter echoing, memories keep.
In every bite, a chuckle found,
In joyful hearts, love knows no bounds!

Seasons for Sowing Thanks

As springtime wakes the sleepy seeds,
They giggle, rolling, oh such leads!
With sun hats made of leafy greens,
They plot their pranks, oh what routines!

Oh, the carrots wear a funny hat,
While broccoli dances, think of that!
The radishes blush, feeling shy,
While beets puff up, oh my, oh my!

Summer shines on ripe delight,
Giggles rise with each bite taken right.
Zucchinis long, like jokes they stand,
On friendly shouts from garden land.

As autumn spills her golden cheer,
We gather all, hold friends so dear.
In every bowl, a silly tale,
From fields that laugh, our thanks unveil!

The Comfort of Crops

In cozy corners, veggies settle down,
As the onions joke, don't make a frown!
Potatoes whisper secrets in the muck,
While radishes prance, oh they're out of luck!

Tomatoes throwing juicy jibes,
As peppers dance in vibrant tribes.
The harvest brings both giggles and glee,
A veggie troupe, singing joyfully!

In baskets piled, a comic scene,
Corn on the cob, so sweet and keen.
With every nibble, laughter breaks,
With hearty meals that friendship makes!

So when the sun sets on our fields,
And laughter pains, the joy it yields,
With every bite, we smile and munch,
Life's quirks harvested, it's quite the punch!

Echoes of Fertility

In the fields where veggies dance,
The corn has taken quite a stance.
Tomatoes blushing, oh so bold,
Claiming glory, green and gold.

Pumpkins plotting in a row,
Saying, 'We're the stars of the show!'
With each sprout, a giggle sprouts,
Nature's whimsy, no doubts about!

A cabbage wearing a crown of leaves,
Ruling over peas, like playful thieves.
Carrots hide in their earthen beds,
While broccoli whispers to the threads.

So let's give thanks with a chuckle loud,
For every veggie, we are proud.
Let's toast with juice from sunny fruit,
Nature's laughs, oh, what a hoot!

Serenity in Every Seed

Seeds tucked snug in beds of earth,
Dreaming dreams of salads, a time of birth.
Each tiny capsule whispers sweet,
'Grow me big, oh what a treat!'

Sun's warm smile, rain's gentle cheer,
Mighty plants bloom without any fear.
Radishes chuckle as they peek,
'We're spicy snacks, so don't be meek!'

A pea pod jokes, 'I'm a little green bean,'
Twisting on vines, where've you been?
With whispers of joy in the sunny air,
They giggle and wiggle as they share.

So dance with veggies, join the spree,
Harvest laughter, wild and free.
In every seed, a story thrives,
With every bite, the joy arrives!

A Tapestry of Giving

Woven threads of sunshine bright,
Stitching greens, oh what a sight!
Lettuce layered with a wink,
Salads giggle, don't you think?

Beets blush, feeling very bold,
Vowing to never be left cold.
Bees buzz in a cheerful tune,
Harvesting sweetness, morning to noon.

A pie made with apples so sweet,
Crust so flaky, can't be beat.
Everyone gathers with a grin,
For veggies and laughter to begin!

Let's raise a glass to all that grows,
In funny ways, our bounty shows.
Each morsel savored, giggles entwined,
In nature's jest, a joy defined!

From Plow to Table

From plow to plate, oh what a ride,
Veggies trot in with endless pride.
'You're my favorite!' the chef does shout,
As broccoli donks the bowl about.

Carrots parade in their orange suits,
While onions shed tears, oh how they hoot!
A dance of flavors, they take their turn,
For mashed potatoes, their love does burn.

Each bite a chuckle, each taste a cheer,
A feast of joy, all gathered here.
With every nibble, the laughter grows,
As funny happenings in the garden flows.

So let's celebrate with tummies so full,
For nature's gifts, we've cherished, not dull!
Together we savor, giggle, and toast,
To veggies that spark joy, we love the most!

Reap

In fields where veggies wave hello,
The scarecrow dances, stealing the show.
Carrots hide deep, like they're playing tag,
While pumpkins grin, it's a real gag.

The corn stands tall, like a ladder so bright,
Hoping to reach the stars at night.
We pluck and chuck with laughter loud,
As the radishes blush, feeling proud.

Digging up spuds, they tumble and trip,
Potato party, let's all take a sip!
Each harvest haul brings joy and cheer,
We laugh so hard, the neighbors can hear.

Reflect

With baskets full of joy and glee,
We reminisce 'bout that big ol' bee.
Buzzing 'round the blooms, a sweet parade,
Plotting their heist on our honey trade!

The sun above, a cheeky grin,
Warming our backs as we start to spin.
Remember the day we planted our seed?
Now we're buried in veggies, oh what a breed!

Each blink of green, a smile revealed,
Nature's chuckle, a merry field.
Let's toast to blooms and frolic too,
In the garden of giggles, with a great view.

Rejoice

Gather 'round friends, it's time to cheer,
For harvest time is finally here!
Tomatoes rolling like jolly red balls,
While onions giggle at our teary calls.

Spinach and lettuce in a leafy dance,
Try to eat them, if you dare take a chance!
The peas are popping out of their pods,
While the broccoli flexes, looking like gods.

We'll roast and toast 'till the stars shine bright,
Under the moon, we'll feast through the night.
In joyful laughter, we'll share our meal,
With a dash of humor, it's the best deal!

The Blessing of Backbreaking Labor

With shovel and spade, we dig and toil,
Turning the earth for a bountiful spoil.
Sweaty brows but spirits high,
Even worms seem to laugh as they pass by.

The weeds, they chuckle at our disdain,
While we sweat it out in the sun and rain.
But oh the joy when we see our prize,
A garden that glistens under blue skies!

Each blisters a badge, each ache a song,
We dance through the harvest, where we belong.
A little craziness under the sun,
In this backbreaking grind, we still have fun!

Sunshine, Soil, and Surprise

Under the sun, with our hats pulled tight,
We dig for treasure, what a delight!
Oh look, a radish that's gone rogue,
Wearing a wig, like a garden vogue!

The soil's a friend, so warm and deep,
As we unearth laughter, not just heaps!
A worm pops up, and takes a bow,
While carrots boast, "We're the best, now!"

Each sprout a giggle, each leaf a grin,
Surprises abound where our roots begin.
In sunshine's glow, we work and play,
With laughter sprouting, come what may!

The Gift of Each Grain

Let's celebrate the stuff on our plate,
Each kernel of corn, isn't it great?
Wheat fields swaying like a dance team show,
Munching on muffins, watching them grow!

Barley's in line for a beer or two,
With hops jumping in, saying, "Cheers to you!"
Each grain's a giggle, ready to bloom,
In the pantry party, there's always room!

So raise a toast to the earth below,
For the funny gifts that help us grow.
With every nibble, remember with glee,
These grains bring us joy, as wild as can be!

Dance of the Ripened Yield

The corn is high, the pumpkins swell,
I tripped on squash, oh what a smell!
The veggies giggle, the fruits they cheer,
The autumn dance brings laughter near.

The farmers twirl in their old galoshes,
Chasing fast chickens, oh how they frolic!
Tomatoes blush while carrots grimace,
It's veggie limbo in this fine place!

Cider spills while apples grin,
A crisp delight now let's dig in!
They all unite for a silly song,
In the golden sun, we can't go wrong.

So raise a glass of pumpkin brew,
To nibbles, sips, and laughs so true!
We toast to fields, they dance about,
With hearts of cheer, there's never doubt!

A Canvas of Thankful Colors

In fields of gold, where laughter grows,
A pumpkin's smile and a carrot's pose!
The sun dips low with a wink and nod,
While veggies burst forth, oh my, how odd!

With kale in capes and beets in boots,
They strut and dance in silly hoots.
A rainbow plate to fill our eyes,
As farmers grin, a delightful surprise!

The peppers jive, the onions spin,
They welcome fall, let the fun begin!
Squash with shades of every hue,
Tickling our taste in a colorful brew.

So let's paint plates with nature's art,
A feast of joy that warms the heart.
In silly shades, let's all partake,
In this harvest season, giggles awake!

Flocks and Fields in Harmony

The sheep are baa-ing in silly tunes,
While roosters strut beneath the moons.
Goats eat hats, and chickens prance,
In this farmyard, we join the dance!

The ducks in line do a wobbly waddle,
While horses laugh at the goat's funny coddle.
The pig with shades takes a nap in hay,
Dreaming of snacks, oh what a day!

The scarecrow tells jokes to all nearby,
While the wind whispers a gentle sigh.
They gather round for a harvest feast,
With laughter and cheer, it's quite the beast!

From fields to flocks, harmony flows,
In this merry gathering, joy only grows.
So cluck and moo, let's make a scene,
In this funny farm, we reign supreme!

Thankful Hearts

With baskets full and smiles so wide,
We carry our treasures with silly pride.
The carrots wink, saying, "Take your share!"
While broccoli bows with graceful flair.

A cabbage rolls like it's on a spree,
Joining the party so merrily!
As corn stalks gossip, they plant a joke,
The harvest fest is no mere poke!

A table set with a jumbled spread,
Cornbread giggling as it's being fed.
With every bite, a chuckle springs,
Thankful hearts for these joyful things!

We cheer and dance with plates piled high,
Underneath the big, blue sky.
So pass the pie, let's share a laugh,
In this harvest time, we find our path!

Harvested Dreams

Beneath the sun's warm, golden beams,
We gather all our wildest dreams.
The fields are ripe, they overflow,
With playful antics, watch them grow!

The pumpkins plot a grand prank spree,
While beans are brewing a pot of tea.
The tomatoes hide with giggles loud,
Ready to shock the unsuspecting crowd!

A scarecrow's dance brings forth loud cheers,
With random moves that tickle ears.
Every harvest is a wondrous sight,
Where laughter reigns and spirits ignite!

So stack the crates and spread the cheer,
As we harvest joy throughout the year.
With funny tales and tasty dreams,
We gather all in these silly schemes!

From Seed to Celebration

In springtime's jest, we plant our dreams,
Little seeds giggle, or so it seems.
They sprout and dance, in the sun's warm hug,
Watch out for weeds, they've got quite the bug!

With water and sun, they grow so tall,
Vegetables chuckle, waiting for the fall.
Carrots wear glasses, quite the funny sight,
But broccoli shouts, 'I'm the veggie of the night!'

Harvest time comes, we bring in the loot,
Pumpkins roll over, saying, 'Here's the root!'
Corn on the cob, wears a smile so wide,
As we feast and laugh, it's a merry ride.

So grab a fork, let's dig in with glee,
As we toast to the crops, beneath the old tree.
Food, friends, and fun, what a delightful mix,
Filling our hearts with nature's sweet tricks!

Honoring the Cycle of Growth

Oh little acorn, what will you be?
Dreaming of branches, as tall as a tree.
With squirrels as cheerleaders, they jump and shout,
'You'll be the best, there is no doubt!'

Spring brings a blossom, a colorful cheer,
Making bees giggle, flitting about here.
Petals in pink, and sunflowers yellow,
Each flower a joke, oh aren't they mellow?

Now summer arrives, oh what a scene,
Tomatoes in stripes, oh so very keen.
Zucchini gets jealous of eggplant's new dress,
And peppers get spicy, causing a mess!

With autumn's big party, we gather 'round,
Eating pies and cake, in laughter we're drowned.
As we celebrate growth, in our funny hats,
Nature's great bounty, and all of its chats!

Tapestry of Autumnal Thanks

Leaves tumble down in a vibrant race,
The trees are giggling, look at that face!
Crisp air fills lungs, as we stomp in glee,
It's the grand finale, come join the spree!

Pumpkins are rolling, 'We're here to stay,'
They banter with squash, 'Hope you're okay!'
Sweet potatoes dance, with roots in the ground,
While apples play tag, circling around.

As we gather harvest, friends share a laugh,
Carving the pumpkins makes quite the craft.
With pies piled high, and cider so bold,
Who thought 'gobble' could ever mean gold?

Raise up your mugs, and let's toast anew,
To every green thing, and to all of you.
In this tapestry woven with color and cheer,
Life's funniest moments, we hold so dear!

Soil Rich with Remembrance

In the earth below, where the worms like to play,
They've got their own show, in a funny way.
With radishes giggling, beneath the ground,
Saying, 'Dig us out, we're treasures profound!'

The spuds have a party, underground they sway,
With dirt as their dance floor, hip-hip-hooray!
Carrots will join, with tops in the air,
But watch your step, 'cause they might just dare!

Come harvest time, we pluck and we cheer,
Every sprout chuckles, bringing good cheer.
On tables, the colors burst forth in delight,
As we munch on this feast, under the moonlight.

So let's give a nod to the soil and sun,
To every little creature, we can't forget fun.
With laughter and joy, let's savor this grace,
Nature's big giggle, in every green space!

Threads of Blessing in Nature's Tapestry

In fields of gold, the corn does sway,
A dance of joy, come what may.
Bunnies munch on patches wide,
While chickens plot their next great ride.

The farmer laughs, his hat askew,
Chasing goats, oh what a view!
With every crop that fills his hands,
He dreams of cheese from far-off lands.

Tomatoes blush, they're quite the show,
Fancy hats upon each row.
Zucchinis try to take the lead,
But squash is plotting, oh yes indeed.

And when the harvest moon does glow,
The veggies laugh, they steal the show.
With every gift from seed to plate,
We raise a toast, oh how great fate!

Gathered in Gratitude

With baskets full, we gather round,
A gathering of joy profound.
Pumpkins pose in orange cheer,
While peas play tricks, oh dear, oh dear!

The apples grin, so red and sweet,
Dancing jigs with wiggly feet.
Carrots pull their leafy hats,
And sing out loud, like chatty cats.

Beans have jumped into the fray,
Declaring, 'Eat us every day!'
While cucumbers, with shades so bright,
Swear they'll keep you feeling light.

So here we sit, with laughter clear,
Eating pie, and sharing cheer.
With every bite, a funny tale,
Of nature's gifts, we shall regale!

Feast of the Earth

A feast is spread upon the ground,
With silly hats and giggles abound.
The potatoes roll with glee,
While broccoli does stand a-twee.

Tomatoes throw their seeds around,
In playful jest, they make a sound.
Corn whispers secrets, oh so sly,
As moths fly by, saying, 'Oh my!'

The pie is bubbling, crust all golden,
While pickles polish, crispy and bolden.
Garlic cloves in little shoes,
Breakdance like they've got the blues.

And as the sunset paints the sky,
We feast and laugh, oh me, oh my!
With every bite, our smiles wide,
Nature's love, we can't abide!

Blossoms of Thanks

Amid the blooms, the colors bright,
Bees hold court, what a sight!
Sunflowers strike their funny pose,
As daisies giggle in sweet rows.

Grateful stems do sway and dance,
Roots tap along, in a flowery trance.
Petals whisper jokes on the breeze,
While lilacs blush, oh, what a tease!

The dew drops cheer, they sparkle and shine,
Like tiny disco balls, so divine.
Each blossom bows with colorful flair,
Declaring joy, floating in air.

We gather round this vibrant scene,
With laughter echoing, sweet and keen.
In every bloom, a chuckle sparks,
Nature's weird and wondrous marks!

A Symphony of Golden Fields

In fields so bright and full of cheer,
The corn grows tall, we laugh and cheer.
We dance with bags and ride on hay,
While veggies plot their getaway.

The pumpkins wink with orange smiles,
As critters raid our veggie piles.
The carrots hide, just like shy kids,
And peas in pods pull funny bids.

The sun can't stop its shining spree,
With every crop, we shout with glee.
The harvest song we sing and play,
We hope no deer will spoil our day.

Our baskets full, we strut around,
With veggies big that almost drown.
In golden fields, we raise a toast,
To nature's jokes, we love the most!

Praise for the Giving Earth

Oh thank you, Earth, for fruits and greens,
With every bite, we hear your beams.
The peas are giggling in their pods,
And garlic's breath gives us the odds.

From tomatoes round to squash that's fat,
We tip our hats to where they're at.
But watch out for that sneaky crow,
He's planning chaos, don't you know!

The apples hang like little moons,
They whisper tales of summer tunes.
We gather up in joyful bands,
With sticky fingers and full hands.

So here's our toast, oh soils and rains,
You keep it fun amidst the pains.
With every bite, we dance and sway,
Thanking you in our funny way!

Gentle Hands of the Land

With hands so gentle, we dig and sigh,
Planting seeds as dreams pass by.
As carrots poke out with a grin,
We crack up, hoping they're not thin.

The lettuce waves, it wants to play,
While radishes hide, just a tad afraid.
We water with love, and chuckle aloud,
As chickens strut and feel so proud.

In this patchwork quilt of green and gold,
The tales of veggies are often told.
We share the laughs, a bowl of stew,
While guessing what they might think too.

So let's embrace the cooler days,
With soup and laughter, in fun-filled ways.
Gentle hands that harvest glee,
Together we grow, you and me!

Echoes of the Harvest Moon

Oh moon so bright, you watch the show,
While veggies dance beneath your glow.
The squash throws shadows, what a sight,
They're laughing hard through harvest night.

The stars are prancing with delight,
As pumpkins swap their names in flight.
With every nibble, comes a cheer,
Of corn and beans that unite here.

The night is filled with cheerful sounds,
Of critters scurrying all around.
Yet nature's jokes keep us awake,
With radish puns, make no mistake!

So raise a glass to moonlit skies,
Where laughter echoes, never dies.
For in this bounty, we all find grace,
With funny farms, life's a merry place!

Milton Keynes UK
Ingram Content Group UK Ltd.
UKHW021940121124
451129UK00007B/163

9 789916 943649